DIVING WITH SHARKS!

And More True Stories of Extreme Adventures!

Margaret Gurevich

NATIONAL GEOGRAPHIC

WASHINGTON, D.C.

Since 1888, the National Geographic Society has funded more than 12,000 research, exploration, and preservation projects around the world. The Society receives funds from National Geographic Partners, LLC, funded in part by your purchase. A portion of the proceeds from this book supports this vital work. To learn more, visit www.natgeo.com/info.

For more information, please visit www.nationalgeographic.com, call 1-800-647-5463, or write to the following address:

National Geographic Partners
1145 17th Street N.W.
Washington, D.C. 20036-4688 U.S.A.

Visit us online at
www.nationalgeographic.com/books

For librarians and teachers:
www.ngchildrensbooks.org

National Geographic supports K–12 educators with ELA Common Core Resources. Visit natgeoed.org/commoncore for more information.

More for kids from National Geographic:
kids.nationalgeographic.com

For information about special discounts for bulk purchases, please contact National Geographic Books Special Sales: ngspecsales@ngs.org

For rights or permissions inquiries, please contact National Geographic Books Subsidiary Rights: ngbookrights@ngs.org

Art directed by Callie Broaddus
Designed by Ruth Ann Thompson

Trade paperback
ISBN: 978-1-4263-2461-1
Reinforced library edition
ISBN: 978-1-4263-2462-8

Printed in China
16/RRDS/1

Table of CONTENTS

DAVID DOUBILET AND JENNIFER HAYES:
DIVING WITH SHARKS!

Photographer David Doubilet comes face-to-face with some Caribbean reef sharks.

A tiger shark feeds on a dead sperm whale.

Chapter 1

FACE-TO-FACE

The radio on the boat crackled to life. David Doubilet and his wife and diving partner, Jennifer Hayes, listened closely. A dead sperm whale had been sighted off the reef of Cairns in Australia. This was rare. There had not been a sperm whale carcass sighting in 30 years. Ten large tiger sharks were feeding on the whale. David knew they had to photograph it.

It's unusual to see sharks feeding in the wild. Sometimes sharks are hand-fed during tours so tourists can dive and see them. David and Jennifer knew that this natural feeding would be a special opportunity.

They set the boat's coordinates (sounds like co-ORE-din-its) to where the whale had been spotted, and sped along the water as fast as they could. Yet when they arrived at their destination, there was no whale to be seen. The wind and tide had moved it, but where?

David and Jennifer scanned the water. Finally, they saw a large mass floating on the ocean's surface. They breathed a sigh of relief. It was the whale.

The whale's white flesh was oozing whale oil. The strong smell filled the air.

And eight large tiger sharks circled the carcass. It was time for David and Jennifer to get a closer look.

David and Jennifer slipped into the water. From there, they had a much better view. The sharks' teeth ripped into the whale's body, tearing it to shreds. David and Jennifer raised their cameras and began taking pictures.

They knew that as long as they kept their distance from the sharks, they'd be safe. After all, the sharks were busy eating the whale. But they had taken some precautions (sounds like pree-COSH-ens), just in case. Both were wearing full diving gear. "We always wear full wet suits, including gloves that cover our hands," said Jennifer. "Our bare hands look a lot like dead fish and may be tempting to a shark used to seeing dead fish as food." They also had their cameras. In some ways, those big cameras helped the team feel safer. It was like having an extra layer of protection between them and the sharks.

So, David and Jennifer focused on shooting pictures. The sharks focused on their meal. In fact, the sharks didn't seem to notice David and Jennifer at all.

But as they kept taking pictures, David and Jennifer didn't realize they were getting closer and closer to the tiger sharks and their carcass. The sharks noticed, though. Suddenly, the mood changed.

The sharks were interested in the two humans bobbing in the water.

David and Jennifer looked around. They had somehow drifted too close to the whale. Now, the sharks saw them as a threat. Finding food in the ocean can be hard, and sharks will protect their meal. David and Jennifer weren't safe anymore.

The sharks began to circle. They swam close enough to bump into David and Jennifer. That's when the photographers thought about their "extra layer of protection." They held their cameras in front of them to block the sharks.

Suddenly, one of the sharks lunged forward. It bit at one of the large, round strobe lights attached to the cameras. Other sharks did the same.

Working Together

David and Jennifer are married, and they work together, too! On land, they have different jobs. David prepares their camera gear and lights. Jennifer researches their subjects and talks with experts. Underwater, they work as a team. To make sure they understand each other underwater, they use hand signals. Or they write using a dive slate and pencil. In dangerous situations, David and Jennifer wear face masks with voice gear so they can talk to each other—that's the clearest form of communication.

Strobes are normally used to light up dark areas. But now they were being used as shark shields!

David and Jennifer needed a way to fend off the sharks until they could swim to safety. They changed their position in the water and put their backs against each other. This way they could see all around them. They could see where the sharks were. That would keep them safe.

They began to swim slowly away from the sharks and toward their boat. The key was to keep their movements small. If they moved too quickly, the sharks would react.

Soon, they put space between themselves and the sharks. That seemed to work. No longer thinking someone was after their food, the sharks headed back toward the whale to finish their meal.

The danger had passed. David and Jennifer shook off the scary encounter. They raised their cameras again to take more photos.

The sun was beginning to set. Dawn and dusk are prime feeding times for sharks. The water was full of the smell of whale oil. That smell brought more tiger sharks to the whale.

David and Jennifer were still in the water taking pictures. But they and their gear were now covered in whale oil.

"Our rubber suits sucked up and absorbed all the whale oil," said Jennifer. "We smelled like food. Like wounded fish."

The tiger sharks were still hungry. Before long, they surrounded David and Jennifer. The sharks made fast runs toward them, bumping and nudging them. David and Jennifer looked to their boat. So did the sharks. The boat was also covered in whale oil. And like the whale, the boat was white.

"It was time to get out before things got out of control," said Jennifer. David and Jennifer swam as fast as they could. The sharks followed. Reaching the boat didn't mean they were safe, though. The sharks tried to bite the boat. David and Jennifer put the boat into gear and motored away as fast as they could.

Jennifer Hayes took this picture of a mother harp seal nuzzling her baby.

Chapter 2

SWIMMING With SEALS

The water temperature in Canada's Gulf of St. Lawrence was below freezing, but diver, scientist, and photographer Jennifer Hayes hardly noticed. She had thick, warm clothes under her dry suit. She wore special dry gloves and boots attached to her suit. These items were made to keep her warm. What Jennifer didn't know was that they would save her life on this dive.

Jennifer was snorkeling alone this time, without her husband, David Doubilet. Her goal was to take photos of a baby harp seal and its mother. But that was a challenging assignment (sounds like ah-SINE-ment) because mother and pup harp seals don't stay together long. After a harp seal is born, its mother nurses it for between 12 and 15 days. Then the mother leaves her pup to survive on its own.

Jennifer jumped into the icy waters in search of a mother and her pup. Before long, she spotted a baby seal on top of a sheet of frozen ice, or ice floe (sounds like FLO).

Just as Jennifer approached the pup, its mother swooped past Jennifer and swam toward her pup. Jennifer watched as the pup and mom met underwater. They rubbed noses. "It was a kiss of recognition," said Jennifer. She captured the tender moment with her camera before the mom led her pup away.

Jennifer wanted more photos of the mom and pup together. As the seals swam toward another ice floe, Jennifer swam alongside them. The pup kept swimming toward her. He seemed interested. But each time the pup got too close, his mom would push him back with her flipper.

Yet the baby seal was determined. As the seals and Jennifer swam through the ice, the pup came closer and closer to Jennifer. When Jennifer and the seals

By day 15, harp seals can reach 80 pounds (36.3 kg). However, after their mothers leave them, they can lose more than half of that weight before they figure out how to survive on their own.

stopped to rest, the pup climbed onto Jennifer's arm. Jennifer floated on her back, and the pup pushed himself onto her chest. Jennifer couldn't believe she was so close to the pup. She clicked away with her camera. Finally, the pup rolled off her chest. His mom swam over and inspected him, making sure he was okay.

Jennifer floated in the water, watching the seals, when she suddenly felt a nip on her right ankle. Then she felt another bite on her left ankle. What was going on?

"I looked down and saw more than 20 male harp seals circling below me," said Jennifer. She took a picture of them. She wasn't worried. She remembered her guide's warning when she was learning to dive: *Sometimes the animals will test you.*

Her thought was cut short, though, as a 400-pound (181-kg) male seal suddenly climbed onto her back and over her head. He pushed her completely underwater and knocked off her mask.

The uncertainty of what could happen next concerned Jennifer. Would the harp seal attack her again? Jennifer grabbed her mask and tried to put it back on her face. Then another blur zoomed past her.

But this blur wasn't after Jennifer. It was the mother harp seal, and she was after the male. The mother seal dived down and slammed into the male seal. Jennifer saw a jumble of fur and flippers as the mother harp seal battled the male seal. Jennifer and the pup floated above the mother and male, watching and waiting.

You Can Be a Diver!

Think you have what it takes to be a diver like David and Jennifer? You can start by watching the animals you want to study. Learn about their habits from the Internet, books, or visiting them in an aquarium. Learn to swim or snorkel. Then bring your camera and practice taking pictures of animals from a safe distance away. Don't be afraid to ask an expert's advice. And be patient. David and Jennifer sometimes wait for hours to get that perfect shot.

Finally, the mother resurfaced. She grunted as she swam toward her pup. She inspected her pup. She nudged him through the water with her head and flippers.

When the mother was sure her pup wasn't hurt, she swam to Jennifer. This surprised Jennifer. She couldn't believe the mother seal seemed to care about her, too. "She began to nudge me like she did her pup, until I was next to him," said Jennifer.

Then the mother began to move the pair through the water, away from the male seals below them. There was a small gap in the ice. The mother and pup slipped into the gap and disappeared. Jennifer watched them go.

Jennifer swam to the edge of the ice and began taking off her weight belt and camera. But before she could finish, she felt a sharp pain on her leg. The male harp seal had returned.

He bit Jennifer again on her thigh. The bite was deep. She knew she had to make it out of the water and onto the ice. If she didn't, the results could be deadly. "He could have pulled me underneath the sheet of ice that went on for hundreds and hundreds of feet," said Jennifer. "I would have been stuck under the ice."

Jennifer jumped onto the ice floe. She could stand on the ice, but it hurt to walk far. Her right leg felt weak, and there were puncture wounds in her dry suit, but there was no gushing blood. "I thought it might not be so bad," she said. But she needed to be sure. Back on her boat, she inspected her leg. The bite was long but not bleeding too badly. It hurt, but it wasn't a life-and-death situation (sounds like sit-yoo-A-shun).

More than two years later, Jennifer still has the scars and the memories. "The suit saved my life," she said. If the suit hadn't been made of tough Kevlar, the seal might have broken through it. Her injuries could have been much worse.

But that frightening moment is not what she focuses on. Instead, she's in awe of the mother seal and how she protected Jennifer. "Had someone else told this story to me, I wouldn't have believed them. I'm less of a skeptic now. Animals do amazing things, and there's no answer why," she said.

David Doubilet captures
the moment when a great
white shark approaches
a diver in a shark cage.

Chapter 3

Great White BITE

It was a beautiful day on the South Neptune Islands of Australia. Rays of sunlight streamed through the clear, blue water. David Doubilet was here to take photos of great white sharks—the largest predatory fish in the sea. David didn't know it yet, but his encounter with one great white would be an adventure.

David has a lot of respect for what he calls "the ultimate shark." He marvels at their size and strength. He wanted his pictures to capture their intensity.

He climbed into a metal shark cage. This would be the only thing that came between him and a great white. His crew helped lower the cage 55 feet (16.8 m) below the surface.

The cage touched the ocean floor. David was glad divers don't wear flippers inside the cage. Without them, he had more room to move around. His camera was large—about the size of a microwave—so he needed the space.

David peered out through the metal bars. The ocean floor was white. Green seaweed and algae (sounds like AL-jee) swayed back and forth on the sandy bottom.

This is a good scene for a picture, David thought, *except the bars are in the way.* He opened the cage door and stepped onto the sand. Now he had a clearer view. The algae-covered sand felt like carpet under his dive booties. David reached back with his foot to feel for the cage. "You always need to know where the cage is," he said. "It's like stealing a base in baseball. You edge out and edge out, but always know where the base is."

With the cage safely close behind him, David lay down in the kelp and began taking photos. A faraway image caught his eye. It was the shape of a torpedo. The top was gray, but the underbelly was white. The underbelly, of course, is what gives the animal its name. David knew: It was a great white shark. David focused his camera and took a photo from his spot on the ocean floor. This shark was big. It was still far away, but he guessed it was about 14 feet (4.3 m) long and weighed about 1,800 pounds (816 kg).

David wasted no time. He stood up and took a few more images. The shark swam a little closer. David clicked his camera again. The shark came even closer. David wasn't scared. From behind his camera, it was easy to forget that he was inches away from one of the ocean's greatest hunters.

Before he knew it, the shark was swimming around him through the sea grass. The shark was getting more aggressive by coming so close. David knew he needed to get back in his cage. But he wanted just one more shot. *Click*. Then he moved his foot behind him. He couldn't feel the cage. Keeping his eye on the shark, he stepped farther back and felt around again. Nothing.

That's when he saw it out of the corner of his eye. The cage was about 50 yards (46 m) away. A wave had lifted and dragged the boat when David wasn't looking. David was face-to-face with a great white shark and had nowhere to go for cover.

David tried not to panic. He needed a plan. He just had to swim slowly and carefully toward the cage. With his gear in tow, he got ready to swim for it. That's when he realized he had another problem. Without flippers, it was hard to swim. The great white moved in closer. Swimming away calmly wasn't an option now. Now David needed a shield. All he had was his large camera. He raised it. This time, it wasn't to take a picture. This time, it was to protect himself.

David kept his eyes on the shark and stepped back with his foot. The shark followed. David pushed his camera against the shark's nose. The shark darted away.

David took another step back. But without his flippers, he couldn't get a good grip on the sand. "It was as if you were in big, white socks and trying to run on a polished wooden floor," he said. He was getting nowhere fast.

Sharks in Danger

Some people may fear sharks, but sharks have a very important role in the food chain. If they disappear, our ocean ecosystem will become unbalanced.

Here's how you can help:

1. Learn about sharks by going to an aquarium or library.

2. Say no to shark fin soup. Removing a shark's fins and then leaving it to die has resulted in a loss of as many as 100 million sharks a year.

3. Check out Shark Angels, an organization focused on getting kids involved in shark preservation, to see what more you can do. (sharkangels.org)

In seconds, the shark returned. David stepped back again, but the shark moved toward him. He lifted his camera and pushed it hard against the shark's nose. Again, the shark darted away.

"I was walking and hopping in wet suit booties," said David. "Every time the great white got closer, I pushed him away with the big and heavy camera."

David spotted the cage out of the corner of his eye. He was closer to it now. How many more steps would he need to reach it? Ten? Twenty? He needed more time to get to the cage.

This time, as the shark approached, David pushed his camera into its nose much harder. The shark moved back. So did David, closer still to the cage.

David reached behind and this time, he felt the metal bars of the cage on his fingertips. His fingers wrapped around the bars as he pulled himself inside the cage. He slammed the door shut.

And just in the nick of time. Now the great white was barreling toward him with its mouth wide open.

The shark rushed the cage at full speed. David stepped back and began to shoot photos just as the great white slammed into the metal bars. Luckily, David's grace under pressure helped him avoid disaster— this time.

"What I want to do is make pictures," said David. "The idea of being frightened gets pushed aside." The danger hasn't stopped him from swimming with sharks.

Deep-sea diver Rhian Waller gets ready for a dive.

RHIAN WALLER:
KEEPING
YOUR COOL!

Rhian Waller battles icy waters when she dives.

Chapter 1

COLD Conditions

Rhian (sounds like ree-ANN) Waller is a cold-water diver and is used to freezing water temperatures. As a deep-sea ecologist (sounds like ee-KAH-luh-jist), she studies living things in water. Her passion is corals. *Desmophyllum dianthus,* in fact. These are hard to find, though. Which might explain why she risks life and limb to see some.

What is *Desmophyllum dianthus*, exactly? It's a type of cold-water coral. Corals are ancient animals related to jellyfish and anemones. An individual coral is known as a polyp (sounds like POL-ip). A polyp is a very small and simple creature. It's an invertebrate (sounds like in-VUR-tuh-brit), or an animal without a backbone.

In some ways, a polyp is little more than a stomach and a mouth with tentacles! A polyp stretches out its tentacles to sting and then eat tiny organisms called plankton.

When thousands of polyps live together, they form a colony. As each polyp grows, it leaves behind its exoskeleton, or hard outside covering.

Over time, the skeletons of many coral colonies add up to build a coral reef. Many species (sounds like SPEE-sheez) of fish and marine life make their homes on and around these reefs.

Coral reefs are found all around the world in warm tropical and subtropical oceans. They are usually found in shallow areas. But in some cases, coral reefs survive in deeper and colder places.

Rhian wants to understand animals that live in extreme conditions, like cold-water corals. How did they get there? How do they continue to live there? How do they survive changes in their climate?

But studying these creatures isn't easy. To study them, you have to go to where they are. And that means searching for them by diving into the dark and freezing waters where they live.

On one of her diving trips, Rhian had gotten lucky. She'd learned that the corals she was interested in had been spotted near Chile. So she traveled to Chile to see for herself. She was not disappointed.

She found many healthy corals in the coastal waters. She and her teammates wanted to study this area, so they set up an underwater lab there.

They tagged corals by attaching sensors to them. The sensors would track the temperature of the water. They would also track how salty the water was and how much light the corals received during the day.

This was important information that Rhian and her teammates needed. The data from the sensors would help them learn more about how corals and other living things survive in these cold waters.

Now, a year later, Rhian and her teammates had a narrow window to visit the spot again. This time, she would replace the old sensors with new ones. She just needed the weather to cooperate.

Rhian and her team set out on a boat toward the corals. But fierce winds blew and a heavy rain pelted their faces. Rhian was already cold, and she hadn't even gotten out of the boat.

The water temperature would be a chilly 55°F (13°C). That was too cold for regular scuba gear. She'd need plenty of layers and a dry suit.

Rhian sighed. This wasn't ideal. Dry suits are big and baggy. But cold-water divers need the extra room so they can dress warmly underneath.

For a dive under these conditions, Rhian would typically wear a lot of layers—including long underwear and fleece clothing. A dry suit had to fit over everything. A ready diver looked pretty bulky. "It's like you're wearing a plastic bag," said Rhian. "And they're clumsy to dive in."

Still, it was much better to be clumsy than cold. If she got too cold, she would be at risk of hypothermia (sounds like hi-poe-THUR-mee-uh).

It can be a life-threatening condition. It happens when the body loses heat faster than it can produce heat. A diver's body

Did You Know?

A human's normal body temperature is around 98.6°F (37°C). When your body temperature drops below 95°F (35°C), hypothermia can set in.

temperature drops dangerously low. If the body temperature stays too low for too long, the heart, nervous system, and other organs can't work properly.

Once in the water, she knew she'd only have 30 minutes of dive time before getting too cold or running out of air. Was it enough time?

Rhian had another worry, too. With all the wind and rain, the water had become very choppy.

Small waves churned up the sand on the seafloor. This would make the water murky. Would she be able to see well enough to find the corals? Or would her trip be wasted?

pink-tipped surf anemones off Vancouver Island, Canada

Living With Corals

Coral reefs come in all shapes, sizes, and colors. They are often described as the "rain forests" of the ocean because, like rain forests, they are some of the most diverse ecosystems in the world. Thousands of plants and animals make their homes there. Experts think nearly one-third of all ocean fish species live part of their lives in or near coral reefs.

Not all coral reefs are found in tropical waters, though. Believe it or not, many coral reefs can be found where the water is icy cold and there is little or no light. But that doesn't mean they have any less life. In fact, scientists have discovered nearly as many kinds of deep-sea corals as shallow-water corals!

Cold-water corals are important to ocean life. Animals such as worms, sea stars, lobsters, and fish depend on deep-sea corals. The corals offer food and places to hide from predators. They also serve as good hiding places for young sea creatures to grow up safely.

Rhian Waller and her teammates enter the icy water.

Chapter 2

DANGER in the DARK

Rhian and her two diving partners grabbed their flashlights, headlamps, and air tanks. They set their timers and dived into the icy water. Even with their dry suits, the cold water sent shocks through their bodies. They had 15 minutes to find and tag the corals. After that, they had to head back to the surface because they could run out of air.

As they dove into a fjord (sounds like FEE-ord), Rhian peered through the water around her. A fjord is a long, deep, narrow body of water that is surrounded by land on three sides. Fjords have steep sides, and corals can grow along the walls.

The driving rain and wind had stirred up a lot of sediment, or bits of sand and other things, in the water. Rhian had expected the water to be murky, but it was worse than she imagined.

Less than three feet (1 m) below the surface, Rhian and her diving partners had to turn on their headlamps to see. They also did a buddy check to make sure they were all still together. Despite feeling uneasy, everything seemed in order.

They dived deeper. The water grew darker and darker, but they needed to keep going. Rhian and her team knew to look for the corals between 90 and 100 feet (27 to 30 m) below the surface. They swam down 20 feet (6 m), then 40 feet (12 m), then 60 feet (18 m). They passed mussels and algae. No sign of corals yet in the muddy, thick water.

Finally, they reached the right spot. Rhian looked around for a large fishing net. When she had been there the year before, she and her team had placed the net around some corals. They had attached the sensors to the net. But where was it? She couldn't find it now.

Rhian grew worried. The clock was ticking. She tried to stay calm, but she was beginning to panic. Where was the net? And where were the corals? She and her diving buddies flashed their lights about, looking. Suddenly one of the beams lit up a clump of corals. They were sticking out ten inches (25.4 cm) from the wall.

They were beautiful. In the dim light, Rhian could see their brilliant colors. They were pink, orange, and yellow. They were tube-shaped. The tentacles at the end of the tubes were delicate. They looked like feather dusters. And there was the fishing net around them, just as she had left it.

Rhian and her partners swam to the net. It wasn't easy. "We could barely see each other," explained Rhian.

Once they reached the net and corals, they got to work. But the big dry suit made tagging difficult. Dry suits are filled with air. Rhian felt less like a diver and more like a big, helium-filled balloon. She had to be careful. If the bulky dry suit damaged the coral, all their work would be for nothing.

Together, they worked as quickly and carefully as they could in the dark. "It was quite a game to see where to put our hands and secure the ties," she said. "We had to rely on our sense of touch."

Finally, they managed to collect the old sensors and attach the new ones. Just as they finished, their alarms went off. Their time was up. It was time to swim back up to the surface. Yet they had to be careful. Coming up too quickly was dangerous.

Save Our Corals

Corals need our help!

They're endangered. One reason is dangerous fishing methods. Fishermen try to catch as many fish at one time as possible. They want to force the fish to come out into the open water. To do this, they blow up corals. This makes large numbers of fish escape the corals at once.

Another risk to corals is chemicals and fertilizer used in farm soil and home gardens. The chemicals run into the oceans and poison coral. The fertilizer gets into the water, too. It causes more algae to grow. When there is too much algae, it covers the corals, and they die. Even a swimmer's sunscreen in the water can kill corals.

There are a lot of threats to corals, but there are ways to work to save them, too. Walking or biking instead of driving and using less electricity, gas, or oil can help reduce pollution. Also, remember the three R's: reduce, reuse, and recycle. Finally, use your voice. Tell people how important corals are and help them make smart choices, too.

Murky water and low light levels make deep-sea diving challenging.

Chapter 3

RUNNING OUT OF AIR

*D*on't rush, don't rush, Rhian told herself over and over. She had 15 minutes of air left. Would that be enough time to finish their work and return to the surface? They weren't far from the surface, but even so, they couldn't hurry their trip back up. Rising too quickly was dangerous. It could make the divers sick. None of them could risk making this dive worse.

As divers go deeper underwater, nitrogen from the air gets trapped in their blood. Imagine your body is like a bottle of soda. If you open the bottle too fast, it fizzes up and overflows. If you open it really slowly, it doesn't fizz as much. That's how your body works in dives, too.

If the nitrogen escapes too quickly, it can cause a condition called decompression (sounds like DEE-com-PRESH-un) sickness, or "the bends." The bends can cause serious damage. It can tear apart tissues and damage nerve endings.

That's why it's important to go up slowly and stop at different depths. These are called safety stops. They let the nitrogen gas that's trapped in the body gradually dissolve. Without these stops, nitrogen bubbles can form or move to any part of the body.

Divers often first feel the early stages of the bends in their joints. Their arms or shoulders might start to ache. Some divers feel their skin start to itch. In extreme cases, a diver might think there are insects crawling over his or her skin.

The bends can also make a diver feel light-headed or clumsy. This can be especially dangerous because a diver needs to be alert at all times.

If a diver rises too quickly, it can also cause breathing problems. In some rare cases, the bends can be fatal.

Now, on their way back up, Rhian and her teammates looked for warning signs of the bends. They slowly swam upward to their first safety stop. As they rested, the strong current and waves rocked the water. "We were getting knocked sideways and swayed around," said Rhian. "There was nothing to hold on to at this safety stop." The divers huddled together in the water.

In spite of the darkness and jostling, they needed to do a buddy check. Rhian looked to her left. Her first diving partner was there. Just as Rhian felt a sense of relief, a huge wave pushed her.

She quickly looked to her right for her second buddy. He wasn't there.

Rhian felt a rush of fear. She needed to find the other diver. She needed to find him now. Her air was running out, and there wasn't time to waste. But the waves were pushing against her. They were pushing her away from the one buddy she could find.

Before another wave could sweep her farther away, Rhian reached out. She and the remaining teammate grabbed hands. Now they could search for their missing buddy together.

Given the direction of the currents in the water, Rhian thought she knew which direction he might have gone. Every minute spent searching was a minute less of air in her tank, though. As she searched, she tried to focus her thoughts.

She also tried to stay calm. *You can't panic,* she said to herself. If she worried, she might breathe faster and use up her air more quickly. The panic might also make her thoughts become confused.

Rhian's alarm went off again. Now they only had ten minutes of air left. Time was nearly up. She and her buddy would need to keep swimming toward the surface if they were going to make it back safely.

As they swam upward, they scanned their flashlights back and forth below them and to the side, trying to catch sight of their missing partner. But their beams of light were no match for the dark water.

Only five minutes remained on their timer. Rhian couldn't leave her missing buddy behind. But if she stayed much longer, both she and her remaining buddy would die.

Rhian gripped her buddy's hand tighter. They hadn't lost each other. But they hadn't found their teammate, either. They were getting close to the surface now. The timer was counting down. Suddenly, Rhian and her buddy broke through the top of the water.

The rain was still driving down. The winds were still kicking up waves. She frantically looked around.

Then, she saw him. The missing diver was clinging to the wall just above the water's surface.

Rhian felt flooded with a sense of relief. She and the other diver swam to the wall. They joined their missing teammate. Before long, their boat captain had pulled the boat alongside them.

Rhian and her teammates dragged themselves onto the boat. They lay shivering and exhausted but ready for the long, choppy ride back. As they sped along, the missing teammate told Rhian his story.

When he reached the surface of the water, he didn't think he could risk swimming to the boat alone in the choppy waters. So he found something to hold on to. He had been searching for them, too. He had been just as worried and panicked as they were!

Rhian thought about the dive. It had certainly been dangerous. But during the worst moments, she and her teammates had remembered their training. They had looked out for one another and kept each other safe.

Rhian also thought about the corals. Her team had succeeded in their mission. They found the netted corals and collected the sensors. They left behind new tags for new data. She knew this information would be important to their research.

"The more we learn, the more we're realizing just how important deep-sea ecosystems are to life up here on land," she explains. Finding ways to protect these ecosystems has become her goal.

"Everything we do on land is connected to the ocean and is connected to the atmosphere," Rhian says. "We're all in this together, so we all have to change the way we treat this planet of ours." So, yes, the dive was dangerous. It left the team shaken. But it was worth it.

Pristine Seas Initiative

Our oceans are full of life, but that life
needs protecting. Three major threats
to ocean life are overfishing, marine
pollution, and the effects of climate
change on the ocean. That's why National
Geographic Explorer Enric Sala created
the Pristine Seas initiative. His goal is to
protect the last wild places in the ocean.

But Enric wants to do more than just protect the pristine, or unspoiled, areas. He also wants to help restore areas that may have been damaged by humans. Enric hopes to save our seas through education, exploration, scientific research, and the sharing of information between communities and global leaders. By working together, Enric knows we can make a difference.

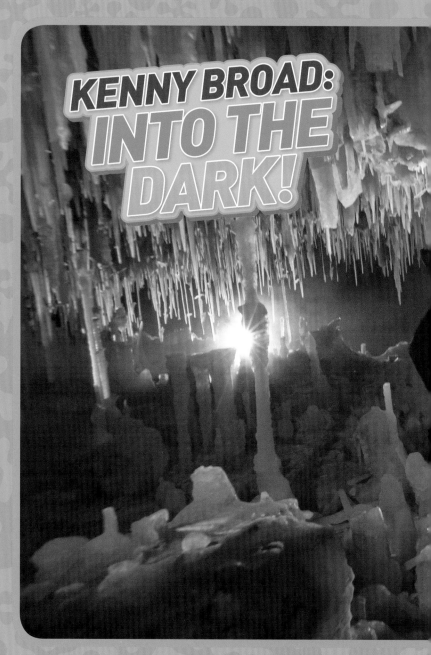

KENNY BROAD: INTO THE DARK!

Kenny Broad makes his way through a narrow passage in an underwater cave.

Kenny Broad shines his flashlight on a mineral formation in an underwater cave.

Chapter 1

DIVING DEEP

Kenny Broad spends a lot of time imagining what can go wrong on a dive. Will there be enough air in the tank? Will there be any light to see by? Will his gear work? He isn't a worrywart. Kenny is an anthropologist (sounds like an-thruh-PAH-luh-jist) and a cave diver. He needs to think about these things if he's going to come back from a dive alive.

An anthropologist is a scientist who studies how humans live. As a cave diver, Kenny looks for fossils and artifacts buried deep in caves that will give him clues about how humans lived in the past.

He's been diving for 25 years. During that time, Kenny's explored many caves. He's wandered through one of the world's deepest underwater caves. It is more than 4,000 feet (1,219 m) deep, in the Huautla Plateau (sounds like WOW-tla pla-TOE) in Mexico. Some of his adventures lead to important discoveries. He dived a cave in Cuba once. There, the team discovered the bones of an ancient sloth!

Yet even with all his experience, Kenny is still cautious. He thinks carefully about each dive. He plans each one with great precision. "You practice thinking through scenarios," he said. "This way, if it really happens, you can respond automatically."

On one dive, Kenny was glad he had imagined the worst. He and his team needed all their wits and training during a dangerous trip through the blue holes in the Bahamas.

Blue holes are huge underwater caves. Many were formed during past ice ages when sea levels were lower and more land was exposed.

This land was made from limestone. Rain wore down the limestone and made holes. Then, as sea levels rose, the holes filled up with water. Now they're underwater caves.

Did You Know?

The deepest ocean blue hole in the world is Dean's Blue Hole of Long Island in the Bahamas. It's 663 feet (202 m) deep.

Blue holes get their name from the color of the water. From above, it looks pure and deep blue. But what lurks below the surface is less inviting. Deadly, even.

Beneath the freshwater is a layer of seawater. This layer is often thick with clouds of poisonous gas. Bacteria that live in the caves make these dangerous clouds. They are no friend to a diver.

The gas can enter a diver's wet suit and seep into their skin. If the diver stays in this layer too long, he or she can suffer from nausea or confusion, or could even die.

And that's not the only danger Kenny and his team would be facing. Swimming against strong currents would be difficult. And encountering underwater avalanches was also a real possibility for the divers.

Despite the dangers, Kenny and his team wanted to make the dive. To them, the payout was worth the peril. There were secrets waiting to be discovered.

For Kenny, blue holes are like time capsules. For hundreds of thousands of years, the Bahamas have been pounded by hurricanes. Much of the land has been washed away, and with it, much of the history of these islands.

But there's one place where the islands' history remains hidden. Buried in the sediment are fossils. These fossils were protected from the storms of the past. Kenny and his team—Nancy Albury, Brian Kakuk, and paleontologist Dave Steadman—hoped these fossils would tell them the story of what lived here long ago.

Blue Hole Preservation

Even though 70 percent of our world is covered in water, only 0.007 percent is available for drinking. That means if you had 16 cups (3.8 L) of water, only a spoonful of that would be drinkable. Blue holes hold some of this fresh drinking water, but they are in danger. People dump garbage inside them. This contaminates (sounds like kuhn-TAM-uh-nayts) the water and the blue hole ecosystem. The Bahamas Caves Research Foundation is working on ways to protect these areas. It wants to make blue holes a "no dumping area" and only allow qualified divers to explore them. Kenny and the Foundation hope these efforts will keep the drinking water and life in the caves safe.

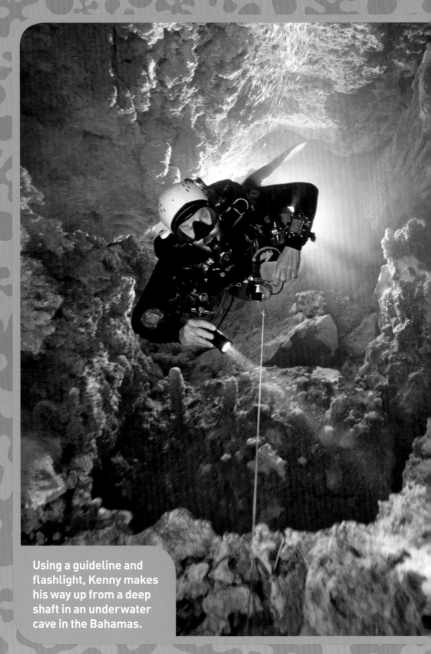

Using a guideline and flashlight, Kenny makes his way up from a deep shaft in an underwater cave in the Bahamas.

On average, ten cave divers die during expeditions (sounds like eks-puh-DISH-uns) each year. Kenny and his team did not plan to be a part of that number. This is why the shakedown dive was the first step of their expedition. The goal of this kind of dive is to make sure all equipment is working. Divers also lay down a guideline through the cave.

A guideline is a rope divers can follow to help them get out of the cave. "You always run a continuous (sounds like kuhn-TIN-yoo-us) guideline from the surface so you can follow it out even if you can't see it, even if visibility is bad," Kenny said. "You put your fingers around it like an OK sign."

But even the guideline can bring danger. Equipment can get tangled up in it. Divers can get tangled in it, too. For this reason, many carry knives to cut themselves free. Most cave divers also carry backup equipment in case of trouble. Kenny always carries three knives, three lights, and a backup air tank.

On this dive, though, Kenny and his team would have to use special scuba devices called rebreathers. Two regular scuba air tanks have less than two hours worth of air in them. Rebreathers would allow Kenny and his team to be underwater for more than three hours at a time.

There are other advantages to rebreathers, too. With regular scuba gear, each breath a diver takes draws fresh air from the tank on his back. When the diver breathes out, the air goes back into the water and forms bubbles. Bubbles can dislodge extra silt from the cave ceiling and make waters murkier. Rebreathers allow divers to breathe their own air over and over. That means they don't make bubbles.

Using rebreathers can be risky, though. They're much more complex than regular scuba gear and take a lot more training to use. The rebreather is supposed to remove the carbon dioxide and provide the diver with fresh oxygen. But if too much oxygen is put back into the tank or the carbon dioxide is not cleaned out properly, the diver is in trouble. A diver can lose consciousness without warning.

Kenny gathered his team for the shakedown dive. Kenny, Wes Skiles, and Brian Kakuk formed the team. Brian is one of the world's most experienced cave divers and the founder of the Bahamas Caves Research Foundation. Wes was a pioneering underwater photographer and Kenny's mentor. Together, they'd be exploring a blue hole called Sawmill Sink.

The divers secured their guideline up top and checked their gear. Their headlamps lit the way as they lowered themselves into the water. They kept one hand on the line and the other hand on the person in front of them. They swam forward slowly.

Suddenly, rocks from the ceiling began to fall down. Sometimes sediment falls from a cave's ceiling and clouds the water. But this was crumbly rock, a result of the soft limestone. It's less common.

Kenny and the others were caught in a massive rock rainstorm. Some divers might panic. But Kenny's training kicked in. He focused on keeping his hand on the guideline and keeping his breathing even. "Once your heart rate goes up," Kenny said, "you start breathing fast and using up air in your tank."

Brian looked for Kenny, but the sediment clouding the water made it hard to see him. Wes couldn't get his bearings. Kenny couldn't read his gauges, but he knew he couldn't stay where he was. "You can't wait it out," he said. "The visibility will stay bad for several hours."

In the darkness, Kenny gripped the guideline and groped at the dark water with his free hand. He caught Brian's leg. Brian, Wes, and Kenny connected and moved along the line.

Finally, they were out of the rock storm and into safety. For a dive that was supposed

Did You Know?

The Bahamas have more blue holes than anywhere else in the world.

to prepare them for the real dive, this one had been eventful. But they had to put it behind them. They needed to focus on what lay ahead. Kenny hoped their real dive would bring some important results.

The Bahamas are 60 miles (96.6 km) off the coast of Florida, U.S.A. Unlike Florida, the Bahamas don't have crocodiles or tortoises. At one time, though, they did.

Kenny and his team were looking for evidence of these lost species. The conditions at Sawmill Sink, where they would start their search, are perfect for preserving fossils.

Finally, the day of the real dive was here. Kenny and his team tested their rebreathers to make sure everything was in order. Then they dove into Sawmill Sink.

Right away, a pink film surrounded them in the water. It was poisonous gas. Kenny and his team knew to expect this. They moved through it fast before it had a chance to seep into their skin.

Once safely through, they saw something by a group of rocks sticking out from the wall. It was an incredible find!

The team discovered a preserved owl's roost, surrounded by thousands of cast-off bones. Kenny and his team carefully collected as many bones as they could find. They couldn't wait to find out their history.

Kenny and his team also found bones of lizards, snakes, bats, and small birds. There was an even bigger discovery, too. They stumbled upon the bones of a tortoise and a crocodile.

Cave Diving Know-How

Swimming through a cave is very different from swimming in open waters. Open-water swimming uses strong kicks and thrusts. This is a cave diving no-no. Mud and fine sediment are big challenges in underwater caves. You want to stir up as little as possible so it doesn't cloud your vision. That's why small, careful kicks are key.

Cave diving can be dangerous. Never go into an underwater cave without proper training and equipment. Here are some other important rules to dive by:

1. Never dive alone.
2. Be in good physical shape.
3. Check your equipment.
4. Come to the surface slowly and with control.
5. Plan your dive and dive your plan.

After carefully collecting all the fossils they could, Kenny and the team resurfaced. The dive went well. But now they had a lot of questions. Kenny had an idea of who could help them find answers.

Nancy Albury and Dave Steadman are paleontologists and two of the world's top experts on island ecology. Ecology is the study of how living things relate to each other and their surroundings on an island.

Nancy and Dave were eager to help Kenny and his team. They first studied all the bones near the owl roost. They discovered the bones were from 46 different species. Many of them are now extinct!

Yet Dave and Nancy thought they knew how these bones ended up in this cave. An owl lived in the cave more than 12,000 years ago. The sea level was lower then. The cave was dry.

The owl would fly in and out to hunt at night. Owls eat their prey whole, but they can't digest bones. Instead, they throw them up. The bones near the roost were from creatures the owl had eaten.

Dave tried to figure out how the tortoise and the crocodile bones ended up in the cave. Bite marks on the tortoise told the story. Dave thought the crocodile ate the tortoise, but wasn't able to make it out of the cave before it died.

Dave and Nancy found a pattern after studying all the animal remains. Most of the species disappeared from the Bahamas almost 2,000 years ago. But why? Kenny and his team were eager to find out.

A diver takes careful notes on the modern cow skull he discovered in an underwater cave.

Chapter 3

A Surprising FIND

Kenny and his team wondered if the disappearance of the animals found in Sawmill Sink might be linked to an Indian tribe called the Lucayans (sounds like luk-EYE-ans). They knew the Lucayans had come to the Bahamas from South America 800 years before Christopher Columbus. They also knew the tribe had a special relationship with blue holes.

In the 1990s, Lucayan remains were found in a nearby blue hole called Sanctuary (sounds like SANK-choo-air-ee).

Kenny and his team decided to go there. They hoped to unlock more of the tribe's secrets. Sanctuary is 260 feet (79.2 m) deep. Dangerous things can happen at that depth, and a diver has to be extra careful.

At that depth, pressure causes nitrogen gas to build up in the blood stream. This can cause nitrogen narcosis (sounds like nahr-KO-sis). Sometimes it can make divers feel too confident and ignore important safety measures. But that's just one set of problems.

Leaving deep waters poses another set of problems. As divers ascend, nitrogen from the air gets trapped in their blood. If they come up too quickly, this can cause a condition called decompression (sounds like DEE-com-PRESH-un) sickness, or "the bends." The trapped nitrogen can cause serious damage to the diver's body.

Kenny and his team made sure they were prepared to dive at Sanctuary. Luckily, explorers have been to this blue hole before. They left their guideline in place. That meant Kenny and his team didn't need to do a shakedown dive. On to the real one, then!

They clicked on their flashlights and followed the guideline down. This time, there was no falling rock, and the water was clear enough to see.

They swam to the area where human remains were discovered years ago. They found them by a sloping ledge at the mouth of the cave. Brian felt something in the sediment. He gently fanned the mud away and pulled out a yellowed human skull. The skull had molars on both sides and one front tooth.

A diver inspects human remains.

They saw indentations on the skull that told them the skull was Lucayan. That's because Lucayans had a practice of wrapping a human head at birth. They placed wooden boards around a baby's head to mold the shape. This made the forehead flat.

No one knows for sure why this was done. Some archaeologists (sounds like ahr-kee-AH-luh-jists) believe the Lucayans thought it made them beautiful. Others believe this forehead shape helped the Lucayans in battle.

The divers collected the skull and other specimens. They wanted to know how old these remains were. They wanted to see if the age matched with the tortoise fossils they discovered in Sawmill Sink.

They would use carbon-14 dating to fill in the dots. Carbon-14 dating is a way for scientists to figure out the age of something that used to be alive.

Keep Calm and Dive On

Remember those "What can go wrong?" exercises Kenny practices before a dive? They're called visualization (sounds like vizh-oo-uh-li-ZAY-shuhn). That's when you imagine something happening and think about how you would react if it did. This technique helps Kenny stay calm. When you're in dangerous cave situations, he says, calmness can be the difference between life and death.

Later, the carbon-14 dating revealed that the skull is 800 years old. The missing puzzle pieces Kenny and his team had been looking for began to come together.

The fossils uncovered in Sawmill Sink dated back thousands of years.

Now there was a bigger mystery. More research showed a gap of about 1,000 years between the youngest found crocodile and tortoise fossils and the oldest found human fossils. What happened between those years?

What could have caused the disappearance of the animals? Dave and

Nancy's theory had been good, but that's the fun thing about science—new data can change what we know and believe. And that means scientists need to keep looking for new answers.

The dangers Kenny and his team faced while diving in the Bahamas were very real. But Kenny doesn't think about that. He only sees each dive as a chance to learn more. Each trip is a way for him to uncover facts about the past. "There are still so many questions. We are just starting to scratch the surface," he says.

THE END

DON'T MISS!

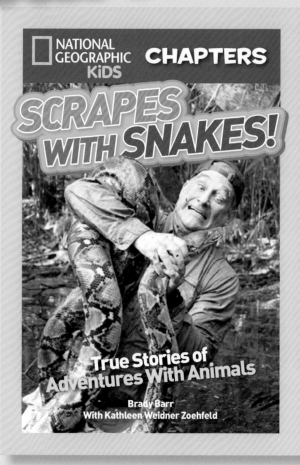

NATIONAL GEOGRAPHIC KiDS **CHAPTERS**

SCRAPES WITH SNAKES!

True Stories of Adventures With Animals

Brady Barr
With Kathleen Weidner Zoehfeld

**Turn the page
for a sneak preview . . .**

Helped by a group of local people, my friend Mark Auliya (third from left) and I show off the reticulated python we caught.

SNAKE
on a
STRING

I spotted this reticulated python slithering off the riverbank into the water. Pythons are great swimmers.

Chapter 1

The Snake PALACE

Years ago, I heard about a mysterious cave on a small island in Indonesia (sounds like IN-doh-NEE-zhuh). The local people call it the Snake Palace. They say that hundreds of snakes live in that cave. And not just any snakes! This cave is home to the longest snake on the planet—the reticulated (sounds like reh-TICK-you-lay-ted) python.

I wanted to see those snakes for myself. So I got excited when my friend Mark Auliya (sounds like eye-OOL-ee-ah), a python expert, told me about his new project. He was going to research big snakes living in caves. The Snake Palace seemed like the perfect place to start. I teamed up with Mark, and we headed for Indonesia.

We flew to a landing strip on a remote island. From there it took us three days to get to the village closest to the cave. A few of the people there offered to lead us to the cave. They took us up and down two mountains. Then I started smelling something really bad. Our guides said the cave was also home to thousands of bats. Bats had lived there for hundreds of years. The horrible smell was from the bat poop!

Finally, I spotted the cave entrance. It didn't look like a palace. It looked like a muddy hole in the rock wall. One of our guides suddenly grabbed my shoulder. He pointed to a bush near the entrance. An angry-looking tree viper stared back at me. We counted six of these deadly snakes in the bushes. Our guides said the vipers are always there, waiting to strike at bats as they fly in and out of the cave.

Our guides warned us that the cave was full of danger. We might meet cobras, scorpions, and giant centipedes. If we survived those, we still had to face all that bat poop, quicksand, and poisonous gases. Mark and I shrugged. We'd come too far to turn back now. We waded in.

The nasty smell made my eyes water. It was all I could do not to vomit. Moving deeper into the cave, I began to hear the high-pitched squeaking of the bats. It sounded like millions of them. We tried to stay close to the cave wall, because that's where the bat poop was less deep. It was already up to our knees.

The farther we went, the more bats we saw. They flapped around our faces. And now the bat poop was waist-deep. It was like wading through a thick soup. The bats were really starting to freak me out, when I saw it: my first reticulated python.

Komodo dragon

leatherback sea turtle

saltwater crocodile

Land of Giants

The country of Indonesia could be called the land of giants—giant reptiles, that is! It is home to the world's longest snake, the reticulated python, and the world's largest venomous snake, the king cobra. Indonesia is also home to the Komodo dragon, the largest lizard on Earth, and the saltwater crocodile, the largest croc on the planet. The world's biggest turtle is also found in Indonesia. It's called the leatherback sea turtle.

The snake was resting on a small rock ledge. It looked about six feet (2 m) long. I reached out to grab it, when Mark yelled, "Snake!" He had spotted one, too. Suddenly the poop smell and the bats didn't seem so bad. We were finding pythons!

Mark and I caught and measured many pythons. The deeper we went into the cave, the bigger the snakes seemed to get. Then I saw a large crack in the cave wall up ahead. I decided to squeeze in and take a look around. Just in front of me, I spotted gigantic coils. Those coils looked bigger around than I am. This looked like a world-record snake.

The only way to know for sure would be to get the snake out and measure it. We decided to tickle and prod the snake with my snake tongs. Maybe that would make it come out. Once it did, we were ready to jump on it and hold on for dear life!

I tickled the big snake. It shifted its coils a little. Mark prodded the snake. Nothing.

After an hour, it was clear to us that the snake wasn't going anywhere. Disappointed, we left the giant snake in the crack and went on with our work. That night we talked about the big snake and decided we'd try again tomorrow.

Early the next morning, we went straight back to the crack. But the big snake was gone! Except for a few bats, the crack was empty. We measured lots of pythons over the next few days …

Want to know what happens next? Be sure to check out *Scrapes With Snakes!* Available wherever books and ebooks are sold.

INDEX

MORE INFORMATION

To find out more information about the explorers and projects mentioned in this book, check out the links below.

sharkangels.org

This is an advocacy and education group dedicated to shark protection.

ocean.nationalgeographic.com/ocean/explore/pristine-seas

Created by explorer Enric Sala, the Pristine Seas initiative was launched to learn more about and help protect the last wild places in the oceans.

bahamascaves.com

The Bahamas Caves Research Foundation is focused on the exploration and conservation of blue holes, underwater caves, and dry caves found throughout the Bahamian archipelago.

coralreef.noaa.gov/resources/links

The NOAA Coral Reef Conservation Program is an international organization working to save coral reefs.

CREDITS

Cover, Jennifer Hayes/National Geographic Creative; 4-5, Jennifer Hayes/ National Geographic Creative; 6, David Doubilet/National Geographic Creative; 12, Jennifer Hayes/National Geographic Creative; 16, Jennifer Hayes/National Geographic Creative; 22, Jennifer Hayes/National Geographic Creative; 26, David Doubilet/National Geographic Creative; 33, David Doubilet/National Geographic Creative; 36-37, Cengage/National Geographic Creative; 38, Julia Johnstone; 46, All Canada Photos/Alamy; 47, All Canada Photos/Alamy; 48, Phoebe Jekielek; 54, Justin Hofman/ Alamy; 55, Jeff Mondragon/Alamy; 56, Phoebe Jekielek; 66, Joseph Clotas; 67 (UP), Cory Richards/National Geographic Creative; 67 (LO), Octavio Aburto; 68-69, Wes Skiles; 70, Wes Skiles; 76, Jad Davenport; 77, Wes Skiles; 78, Wes Skiles/ National Geographic Creative; 87, Wes Skiles; 90, Wes Skiles; 94, Wes Skiles/National Geographic Creative; 96 (UP), Mark Long; 96 (LO), Wes Skiles; 100-101, Brady Barr; 102, Brady Barr; 107 (UP), Barcroft Media/Getty Images; 107 (CTR), Wil Meinderts/Buiten-beeld/Minden Pictures; 107 (LO), Phillippa Lawson/Nature Picture Library; 111, David Doubilet/National Geographic Creative

**To Noah, who waited patiently
for his mom to write a book that interested him.
Hope it was worth the wait, kid!**

ACKNOWLEDGMENTS

I would like to thank Shelby Alinsky for giving me the opportunity to write this book. I really appreciate the vote of confidence. I would also like to thank my editor, Brenna Maloney, for her vision and for working hard to make sure the book met it. Another HUGE thanks to all the explorers I interviewed for this book. David Doubilet, Jennifer Hayes, Kenny Broad, and Rhian Waller took time away from their shark diving, cave exploration, and cold-water dives to patiently answer my questions again and again and again. You all are amazing, and I'm honored to have had the opportunity to interview you. Finally, thank you to my husband and kid who understood the time I had to spend away from them to work, work, work, and work some more on this book. I love you both more than words can ever express.